GET PAID: The Ultimate Quick Guide to getting your customers to pay

Attorney Todd L. Gurstel

and

Attorney Amy Blowers

A MUST-READ for Business Owners, Credit Managers, Collection
Agencies and Accounts Receivables Directors

Hundreds of Dollars in FREE Bonuses Inside

CONTENTS

DISCLAIMER

CHAPTER 1:

WHEN TO ENGAGE A LAWYER TO COLLECT A DEBT

CHAPTER 2:

WHAT EXACTLY IS A JUDGMENT AND HOW DOES IT BENEFIT ME?

CHAPTER 3:

I'VE GOT A JUDGMENT BUT I DON'T KNOW HOW TO COLLECT THE MONEY

CHAPTER 4:

DISPUTE VERSUS DISGUISE

CHAPTER 5:

IF YOU CAN'T AFFORD A COLLECTION LAWYER, YOU'RE USING THE WRONG LAWYER

CHAPTER 6:

INFORMATION THAT IS HELPFUL TO YOUR ATTORNEY WHEN COLLECTING THE JUDGMENT

CHAPTER 7:

TAKING THE LEAP, LEAVING IT TO THE PROS AND PUTTING THE STRESS BEHIND YOU

BONUS

TODD GURSTEL'S 12 STEP PROGRAM

If your business is sitting on receivables and you have said to yourself, "If I could just get my customers to pay up" then this might be the most important book you read all year. Here's why...

Have you ever said any of these statements?

- My business is sitting on receivables but collecting on them seems too complicated.
- Hiring a law firm to collect on my receivables will be expensive.
- My business has taken judgments against non-paying customers, but I don't know what to do next.

Imagine if in just A FEW QUICK STEPS...

Imagine if in just a few quick steps you could finally get paid for the services or products that you provide. You're in luck. *Get Paid* explains how to do that.

In this book you'll discover the following:

WHEN TO ENGAGE A LAWYER TO COLLECT A DEBT-In the first chapter you'll learn the signs that suggest it's time to place your delinquent account with a collection professional and at what age the debt should be before retaining an attorney.

In Chapter 2: WHAT EXACTLY IS A JUDGMENT AND HOW DOES IT BENEFIT ME, we define exactly what it means to have a judgment as well as the incentives to your business that are not otherwise available if it doesn't seek a judgment for the unpaid account.

Next in CHAPTER 3: I'VE GOT A JUDGMENT BUT I DON'T KNOW HOW TO COLLECT THE MONEY, we address a very typical concern clients are faced with when their business obtains a judgment on its own but doesn't have the slightest idea what step to take next to collect on the judgment. We outline the remedies available to Judgment Creditors and the procedure for collecting a debt.

Then in CHAPTER 4: DISPUTE VERSUS DISGUISE, we expose the all-too-familiar stall tactic used by debtors and how to identify when you're being played.

In CHAPTER 5: IF YOU CAN'T AFFORD A COLLECTION LAWYER, YOU'RE USING THE WRONG LAWYER, we demonstrate that hiring an attorney to collect shouldn't break the bank. What to expect when retaining an attorney and the costs that can be added to the judgment balance saving your business money.

CHAPTER 6: INFORMATION THAT IS HELPFUL TO YOUR ATTORNEY WHEN COLLECTING THE JUDGMENT focuses on the documentation that you should send to your attorney to ensure that recovery efforts are successful.

Next in CHAPTER 7: TAKING THE LEAP, LEAVING IT TO THE PROS AND PUTTING THE STRESS BEHIND YOU we discuss the benefits of taking collection efforts off you and your staff's plate and how it can relieve your office of unnecessary stress.

Finally, we share with you a fantastic BONUS: TODD GURSTEL'S 12 STEP PROGRAM FOR COLLECTING JUDGMENTS. Todd presented to a group of collection professionals who paid hundreds to hear him speak at an annual International Association of Commercial Collections Convention. He's sharing it with you just to thank you for your interest in *Get Paid*.

Each of the topics covered in the chapters are equally important if you want to RIGHT A WRONG and get your customers to hold up their end of the bargain, by finally receiving payment from them for the services or product that you provided as promised. Now we'd like to tell you a little about us.

Why should you listen to us?

The bottom line is we are industry experts with a proven system for success and we care! Unlike other law firms who come and go and open under ever-changing names, or who merely dabble in collections amongst multiple other areas of practice, our founding member is a pioneer of debt collection.

Todd Gurstel

Todd Gurstel has focused his practice in collections since 1987. Todd is a recognized leader within the creditors' rights industry, and is known for regularly setting and sharing best practice standards. The firm is highly regarded for its creditor's rights practice, the area in which Todd is passionate. Todd frequently speaks on compliance issues and is a known trade advocate. He has repeatedly received the "Super Lawyer" designation by his colleagues.

Amy Blowers

Director of Commercial Litigation at Gurstel Law Firm, P.C., Attorney Amy Blowers' practice focuses on commercial civil litigation and all related aspects of creditor's remedies for businesses and creditors of all sizes. This practice includes matters related to pre-judgment disputes through post-judgment collection remedies. Amy oversees the collection departments at all our office's six locations. She is admitted before all Minnesota courts.

The Gurstel Law Firm P.C. has offices in Minnesota, Arizona, Iowa, Nebraska, Utah, and Wisconsin and maintains a commercial collections practice nationwide to advocate for unpaid businesses like yours.

Now that we've introduced ourselves and provided you with a roadmap of what you can expect, let's dive right in and make sure you *Get Paid!*

Disclaimer

The information contained in this book is not intended to be used as legal advice and does not constitute an attorney-client relationship with you/your business and Gurstel Law Firm PC, Todd Gurstel or Amy Blowers. Businesses looking to retain collection counsel should contact an attorney who is authorized to practice law in their state. If you don't know an authorized attorney in your state, Gurstel Law Firm P.C. will do our best to provide your business with a reference. Unauthorized use, disclosure or copying of this publication is strictly prohibited and may be unlawful.

CHAPTER 1:
WHEN TO ENGAGE A LAWYER TO COLLECT A DEBT

CHAPTER 1:

WHEN TO ENGAGE A LAWYER TO COLLECT A DEBT

THE LONGER YOU WAIT TO SEND AN ACCOUNT TO LEGAL, THE LESS LIKELY YOUR CHANCES OF RECOVERY

So why do you need to know that the longer you wait the less likely you are to recover? The reason is simple: you want to get paid. The longer you wait to send a past due account to legal, the less likely you are to recover your money. This is true because unless there is a real dispute regarding the account, usually when a customer is not current on one bill, it likely means that they are having difficulties paying other bills as well.

You want to be as far up the food chain as possible. You do this by hiring a lawyer early and then obtaining a judgment before other creditors have the chance to rise above you on the food chain. If you're early enough to the party, there might just be something left to eat. If you're the last one to show up, you can count on starving.

For example, Customer Biz fails to pay ABC Biz and ABC Biz sits on the outstanding account and tries to collect internally to no avail. Several years later, that Customer Biz is defunct, its owner has filed bankruptcy, its bank accounts are closed, it has multiple judgments against it and all of its equipment has been liquidated. There are no longer any assets of Customer Biz. Therefore, ABC Biz will never recover.

To make sure that your business recovers its accounts receivables, you need to send your accounts to legal as early as possible so that you can ensure that your delinquent customer holds up its end of the bargain and finally pays your business the money it deserves.

That's the first bit of information you need to know about the recourse available to your business when a customer fails to pay so that you can finally be made whole.

CHAPTER 2:
WHAT EXACTLY IS A JUDGMENT AND HOW DOES IT BENEFIT ME?

CHAPTER 2:

WHAT EXACTLY IS A JUDGMENT AND HOW DOES IT BENEFIT ME?

Obtaining a judgment against a non-paying customer entitles your business to legal rights and more money than had you not obtained a judgment

This is important for you to know because obtaining a judgment can drive repayment of the debt. A judgment is a court order determining that you are entitled to repayment and ordering your customer to pay you. Once a judgment is obtained, you as the judgment creditor, have the legal ability to garnish bank accounts, go after wages and put liens on property.

All of these legal mechanisms are intended to entice the non-paying customer (known as the "debtor") to voluntarily pay you. If the debtor fails to pay voluntarily, you still have recourse through these legal mechanisms.

Let's say ABC Biz delivers products to Customer Biz and Customer Biz fails to pay the $7,000.00 it owes to ABC Biz for the product it delivered. ABC Biz hires Gurstel Law Firm, P.C. and obtains a judgment against Customer Biz for $7,000.00. Gurstel Law Firm, P.C. then puts a lien on Customer Biz's equipment and goes to its retail store and does a "till-tap" literally removing all cash from the registers! Gurstel Law Firm, P.C. then receives a voluntary check from Customer Biz for the remaining balance due, plus court costs, services fees and garnishment costs and Gurstel Law Firm, P.C. then remits the payment to ABC Biz who is made whole.

That's the second thing you need to know about the recourse available to your business when a customer fails to pay so that they hold up their end of the bargain and finally pay you the money your business deserves. Now let's move to Chapter 3. In Chapter 3 we'll explore what you can do if you've got a judgment but aren't sure what to do next to get paid.

CHAPTER 3:

I'VE GOT A JUDGMENT BUT I DON'T KNOW HOW TO COLLECT THE MONEY

CHAPTER 3:

I'VE GOT A JUDGMENT BUT I DON'T KNOW HOW TO COLLECT THE MONEY

You now understand exactly what a judgment is and realize that it can benefit your business to *Get Paid!* Now we're going to address a common problem our office sees far too often. This is the problem businesses are faced with when they have a judgment but can't figure out what to do next.

We see it all the time. A business owner or credit manager goes to small claims court and obtains a judgment against a customer with a past due account. That's all fine and dandy, but obtaining the judgment is by far the easiest part of the process. It's just the first of many procedural steps a business needs to take to *Get Paid*.

We run into clients who are sitting on hundreds of dormant judgments. Those judgments could be turned over to a collection law firm earning the client money while they work, sleep and play.

Our office frequently represents other law firms who have obtained judgments for non-paying clients or on behalf of their clients, but don't have the knowledge base or interest to take additional steps toward recovering on the judgment.

Judgement execution (the process of getting paid on the judgment) is hugely complex. It is governed by federal laws, state laws and in some cases even local rules of court.

If a party undertakes in execution of the judgment but fails to follow the laws, they risk exposure to liability with penalties that often exceed the amount of the judgment upon which they are seeking to collect.

The process of executing on the judgment varies from state to state and can even vary from county to county. To efficiently and effectively execute on the judgment, the practitioner should have a working knowledge of the procedure and be familiar with the process and the rules.

Our office obtains judgments and executes on judgments throughout the U.S. Our attorneys and support staff have fantastic rapport with the courts and their staff.

Our flagship office is located outside Minneapolis, Minnesota. By example, the following is a list of tasks that one can expect to complete to collect on a Minnesota judgment:

- Skiptrace for a current address
- Perform a UCC check
- Confirm the debtor is still in business
- Do a bankruptcy search
- Do a property/asset search
- Docket the judgment with the court
- In some cases, wait for the stay period to pass
- Obtain a writ of execution
- Locate agents of the business

The list is not exhaustive and is what can be expected in an UNCONTESTED default (the customer doesn't bother to appear for court and therefore a judgment is entered by default) action. If the customer brings a motion to vacate judgment or otherwise challenges the post-judgment procedures, or hires an attorney to remove the action to a higher level court, the procedural process is much more complex.

Some of what are mentioned above are deadline oriented, while some are not.

Some of the remedies available to a judgment creditor include but are not limited to:

- Negotiate an amicable voluntary settlement

- Get the debtor to sign a Confession of judgment (actually avoids docketing of the judgment as long as customer hold up their end of the bargain)

- Serve officers of the business with post-judgment interrogatories

- Perform a post-judgment deposition

- Perform a bank levy

- Perform a wage levy on any personal guarantor (in some jurisdictions there are times when you can obtain a judgment against an officer for failure to respond to a garnishment disclosure)

- Engage the sheriff in conducting a till tap of any cash registers

- Place a lien on real property

- Place a lien on equipment or materials

- Merchant (or third party) lien

- Third party credit attachment

- Seek the debtor's tax return

As you can see, the post judgment execution statutes require a significant knowledge base for businesses wanting to execute on a judgment. The best advice that can be given, is that your business should leave collections to the professionals who take compliance seriously and are less likely to place your business at risk of exposure to liability.

Now you understand the complexity of the post-judgment execution process. You realize that you need to hand off any judgments your business has taken and leave the execution up to an experienced collections lawyer. In Chapter 4: Dispute v. Disguise, we'll delve even further into this process and you'll see what can happen when a debtor presents your business with a big fat hurdle packaged as a dispute.

CHAPTER 4:
DISPUTE VERSUS DISGUISE

CHAPTER 4:

DISPUTE VERSUS DISGUISE

We've introduced you to the complexity of the post judgment execution process and now you can see the importance of retaining an experienced collections lawyer. Now we're going to talk about what to do when you receive a "dispute" from the customer.

When served with a Summons & Complaint directing the customer to appear for a court hearing, the customer has several actions it can take: 1) do nothing; 2) serve your business with a dispute letter or an Answer to the Complaint; and 3) hire a lawyer and bring a counterclaim in response to the claim made against it.

Some assume that if the customer does nothing and fails to appear at the court hearing, that they hit the jackpot because they'll automatically win. As mentioned before, obtaining a judgment is the easiest part of the collections process. It's the recovery of the judgment that is difficult.

If in response to the service of your complaint, the customer serves you with a dispute letter or an Answer to the Complaint, you will need to make a judgment call. You need to determine if the response is actually a dispute or if it is a stall tactic that is merely disguised as a dispute.

It is not uncommon for non-paying customers to get creative and imagine a dispute in an effort to stall payment. If a debtor is getting creative and the dispute is not real, you need to find out why they are stalling. If they're stalling, it could be that they really don't have the money to pay the invoice. You might want to go back to the drawing board and do a UCC check, determine that the business is still up and running, do a judgment search and find out what's really going on.

If you determine that there is a legitimate dispute, you might want to consider settlement. Most law firms who typically offer contingency fee arrangements (you don't pay attorney's fees until they recover on the judgment) will retract their contingency fee arrangement and transition to an hourly fee if a counterclaim is served.

If the dispute is bogus, an experienced collection attorney will evaluate the situation and determine if a motion for summary judgment or a motion for judgment on the pleadings is appropriate. These actions are a good way to obtain judgment on a bogus dispute without expending all kinds of additional costs that are associated with the discovery process.

Now you've got the fourth bit of information you need to *Get Paid*. You understand the distinct difference between an actual dispute and a stall tactic disguised as a dispute. In Chapter 5, we'll talk about what you can expect to pay a collections attorney who handles your past due account.

CHAPTER 5:

IF YOU CAN'T AFFORD A COLLECTION LAWYER, YOU'RE USING THE WRONG LAWYER

CHAPTER 5:

IF YOU CAN'T AFFORD A COLLECTION LAWYER, YOU'RE USING THE WRONG LAWYER

Hiring a law firm to obtain a judgment or collect on a judgment should not be expensive. This is important for you to know because many businesses operate under the misconception that hiring a lawyer to collect is extremely costly. That should not be the case.

A reputable law firm will charge a rate that is unique to the situation of the client as opposed to an industry set rate. Most collection matters can be handled on a contingency basis so the client will not pay for attorney's fees unless the law firm recovers the debt. This type of arrangement encourages the law firm to make smart, efficient and effective decisions when going after a debt.

At Gurstel Law Firm, P.C., we allow our clients to decide when to expend costs. We don't incur costs without the client's authorization.

Finally, most businesses don't realize that many of the costs incurred in the legal process and the collection of the judgment can be added to the judgment balance and eventually recouped from the judgment debtor during recovery of the debt.

Here's a case study: ABC Biz obtains a judgment against Customer Biz for $7,000.00. The underlying contract between ABC Biz and Customer Biz allows for the recovery of collection costs and attorney's fees. When recouping the judgment from Customer Biz, Gurstel Law Firm, P.C. actually obtains a writ of attachment to go after the judgment amount of $7,000.00 plus attorney's fees, plus court costs, plus statutory interest, plus the cost of the writ, plus any garnishment fees incurred, plus process server costs. The amount ultimately recouped from the judgment debtor is $11,130.00.

So now you know that engaging a collections lawyer to help you get paid won't cost you a fortune. In Chapter 6, we'll tell you what information you should provide your lawyer when you retain them.

CHAPTER 6:

INFORMATION THAT IS HELPFUL TO YOUR ATTORNEY WHEN COLLECTING THE JUDGMENT

CHAPTER 6:

INFORMATION THAT IS HELPFUL TO YOUR ATTORNEY WHEN COLLECTING THE JUDGMENT

Now you know that if you are resisting the urge to call a lawyer because you're afraid you'll be billed by the hour, you've hired the wrong lawyer. An experienced collection attorney will bill you on a contingency basis when funds are collected from the past-due customer. In this chapter, you'll learn what information you'll need to provide your attorney once you decide to retain them.

It might sound like a no-brainer, but your attorney needs to see a copy of the underlying agreement. We can't tell you how many times we've seen parties appear in small claims court and tell the judge they had a verbal agreement or made a hand shake deal. That isn't going to cut it. You need a written contract.

It's always good to retain a copy of the original credit application if one exists. This can be helpful for your attorney in obtaining information regarding the business and or the personal guarantor. This information can include where they conduct business, any references, place of business, existing customers, Social Security Number of the guarantor and more.

In a perfect world, you will be able to provide your collection attorney with all invoices related to the account. However, in some cases you can obtain a judgment with the final invoice. Typically this is the charge off statement. In any event, you need to be able to show your attorney the amount due and how you arrived at that figure.

If you have any banking or credit card information your attorney will want that as well. Information regarding where the customer banks and or any merchant accounts (for example you know they have a line of credit with a certain bank or a line of credit in the form of a credit card), that can be advantageous to helping your attorney recover on the debt. Your attorney might be able to perform a third-party levy where he or she can intercept any payments that they may make to a third-party vendor.

Some states have statutes that allow a judgment creditor to pursue a personal guarantee on the underlying contract. In Minnesota for example, if an officer of a business is served with a discovery request and fails to respond, a judgment can be attached to the officer himself. This can be incredibly effective in getting the customer to voluntarily pay. If you have any information relating to the personal guarantor, it's important to provide that information to your collections attorney.

Your attorney will want to know if you've made any efforts internally to collect on the account. This will include communications you had with your customer and or its representatives. If there were any promises made for a payment, your attorney will need to know. If possible, provide he or she with a ledger of the communications you had with the customer.

In-line with any communications you may have had with the customer, your attorney will also want to know where the account lies procedurally. When you retain counsel, let them know if you are retaining them to pursue a judgment, or if you have already obtained a judgment and are hiring them to recover on the judgment. The distinction between the two could result in different quotes as far as what you can expect to pay in your contingency fee to your lawyer.

If you happen to know who your customer's customers are, that's important to your lawyer as well. For example, if your client is a management company and you know that they have tenants who will be paying rent, your attorney needs to know that. He or she may be able to intercept those funds to pay down the judgment balance.

Now you understand the documents you'll need to provide your attorney to obtain a judgment against your non-paying customer. In the final chapter we'll discuss taking the leap to hiring an attorney to assist you with your account receivables. You'll discover what a stress reliever it can be and how it can free you and your staff of countless hours trying to learn a difficult trade for which they weren't hired.

CHAPTER 7:

TAKING THE LEAP, LEAVING IT TO THE PROS AND PUTTING THE STRESS BEHIND YOU

CHAPTER 7:

TAKING THE LEAP, LEAVING IT TO THE PROS AND PUTTING THE STRESS BEHIND YOU

In the previous chapter you learned about the documents you need to provide your attorney when you retain them to collection on any past due accounts. In this chapter, the final chapter, we'll focus on what you can expect when you hire a collections attorney to assist with your accounts receivables.

We've spent countless hours in court rooms. We've seen business owners attempt to represent themselves in small claims court. We've observed businesses who send agents to court on their behalf. Here is what we know: litigation is stressful. It's even more stressful if you don't know what you're doing.

There is a noticeable heavy breathing, clearing of the throat and sweating that can be observed in the courtroom when officers and agents of business are waiting for their case to be called. You can feel the tension when you enter the courtroom. Why stress yourself out when you can pass the baton off to a professional who is well-versed and comfortable appearing at court hearings?

Most judges will require parties to attempt to settle before he or she will hear their case. This means that the business owner, officer or agent of the company will need to go face-to-face and sit down with the nonpaying customer. In many cases, this can stir up a lot of emotion.

Why create all the stress for someone who is being forced to do a job that he or she does not want to do? Pay your employees to do the job for which they were hired and leave the litigation to the professionals.

Preparing for court is a time commitment. Not only are you required to prepare all the materials, but you also need to prepare your case. What will you be offering as far as testimony? Do you have documentary evidence you'll be offering? Did you make copies for the other party and give them an opportunity to review the evidence? What are the facts of your case? What are the legal issues?

All of this requires preparation. Will you be offering the witnesses testimony? Do you need to prepare that? Do you need to prep your witness?

It is not uncommon for us to observe business owners, officers or agents sitting in court for an afternoon or a morning taking them away from their job so they can understand how the court process goes. Few want to go to court underprepared and without knowing what to expect. Because of this, employees spend a day prior to their court date observing the courtroom in preparation for their actual court date.

This is a colossal waste of time, resources and money. Again, leave it to the pros. In most cases, outside of court required costs, you are only required to pay your attorney if your attorney recovers so there is really not much expense to you.

In many states, in order to execute on the judgment you are required to retain an attorney. This is because court rules prevent non-attorneys from signing legal pleadings. So as a business owner, officer or agent, you are precluded from proceeding with post-judgment remedies.

If you are required to get an attorney involved anyway, why not bring them in early so they can use their knowledge to expedite things and get you paid quicker?

Moreover, attorneys have familiarity with court procedures that can otherwise be painstakingly difficult to master. These procedures can vary not only from state to state, but from county to county. As a business owner, officer, agent or employee, you are not regularly performing collection activities and therefore don't have the know-how of a seasoned collections attorney.

What's more, a collections attorney and competent staff have a rapport with the courts, judges and court administration which can facilitate a quicker result.

Now you understand how important it is to take a leap of faith, leave the stress behind you and hire a professional to help you recover on your judgment.

Congratulations! You learned seven important factors that will help your business succeed in collecting on its accounts receivables. We want to thank you for taking the time out of your very busy day to learn about how you can better serve your business and get your customers to hold up their end of the bargain and pay you for the services or products you delivered as promised.

Now you know when to hire an attorney to assist your business to *Get Paid*. You've learned exactly what a judgment is and how it can benefit your business. You understand the next step you'll need to take if you've already got a judgment and want to begin post-judgment remedies. You can now identify the difference between an actual dispute and a stall tactic disguised as a dispute. Further, you realize that hiring a collection attorney isn't expensive. You know what information you need to provide your collection attorney to be successful in recovery efforts. Finally, you understand that litigation can be stressful and that it's in your businesses' best interest, to leave post-judgment execution to a professional.

Now you know what to expect and the course of action you need to take when a customer refuses to pay. With this knowledge, you can arm your business with this information to ensure that you finally right the wrong and get your business paid.

So what do you do next?

If you're looking the easiest, least costly way to RIGHT A WRONG and get your customers to hold up their end of the bargain, by finally getting paid for the services or product that you provided as promised, we want to help you get the results you desire so we've put together a very special no cost, no obligation very limited time offer just for you.

"$300.00 Ultimate Get Paid Planning Session…For Free"

Our commercial collection attorneys have set aside time to personally speak with you and lay out a customized plan for your business so you can RIGHT A WRONG and get your customers to hold up their end of the bargain, by finally receiving payment for the services or product that you provided as promised.

During our time together you will discover:

- *We'll outline a Customized Plan for Your Business Rather than Applying a One-Size-Fits-All plan used by so many law firms, so you'll know the best strategy for recovering your receivables*

- *That we unify the benefits of a Collection Agency and a Law Firm*

- *You don't pay our Fee Unless we Get Your Customers to Pay*

We're so confident that you'll find the "$300.00 Ultimate Get Paid Planning Session-for FREE" so valuable that we're going to give you a…

100% Risk Free Guarantee

Although your consultation is free, we know your time is valuable. We also understand you might be wondering if our offer is as valuable as we say it is so we're putting our money where our mouth is. That's why you don't pay our fee unless we get your non-paying customers to pay you!

Plus, we are offering you these time-limited bonuses absolutely FREE!

BONUS #1

If you meet with one of our attorneys for the $300.00 Ultimate Get Paid Planning Session and decide to retain us, we'll throw in our Asset Search Service for free on every file you place with our firm! This is normally a $75.00/file charge.

BONUS #2

If you meet with one of our attorneys for the $300.00 Ultimate Get Paid Planning Session and decide to retain us, we'll throw in our Judgment and Bankruptcy Search for free on every file you place with our firm! This is normally a $50.00/file charge.

That's $125.00/file savings just for placing accounts with our firm!

Remember earlier in this book when I asked you to imagine if in just a few quick steps you could finally get paid for the services or products that you provide?

We can help you make that happen. The first step is to call our office's 24 hour pre-recorded hotline at (612) 567-2431 that's (612) 56-GET PAID-1 and tell our attorneys you want to take advantage of our offer: "$300.00 Ultimate Get Paid Planning Session…For Free". Or email us at GurstelLaw@gmail.com and we'll set it up!

Sincerely,

Your Commercial Collections Counsel

Gurstel Law Firm, P.C.

P.S. We understand if you're a bit skeptical. Many of our happy clients felt the same way before they met with us but here is what we learned from a couple of our loyal customers:

"We have engaged Gurstel for our collection needs for over eight years now. Gurstel's professionalism and level of detail – not to mention their collection results, have been outstanding!"

- Fred Richards, Johnson Brothers Liquor Co., Inc

"I highly recommend Gurstel Law for all of your media collection needs. I have had the pleasure of working with Gurstel for over 20

years. They are professional, responsive and highly successful at collecting on my behalf. You would be pleased to have them as your partner."

-Brenda Clark , Cumulus Media, Inc.

BONUS

TODD GURSTEL'S 12 STEP PROGRAM

Finally, we'd like to introduce you to an awesome bonus: Todd's 12 step program for collecting judgments. I hope you enjoy it as much as the attendees at the 38th annual IACC conference did. Attendees paid hundreds of dollars to hear Todd speak on this topic.

The System is titled "Todd's 12 Step Program to Collecting Judgments". Although we tease it suggests recovery from addiction, it is specifically geared toward recovery of accounts receivables. We hope you find it helpful in understanding what to expect when executing on a judgment. Here it is:

STEP ONE: Admit we are powerless over our uncollected judgment. Call your customer.

We Admit We Are Powerless Over Our Uncollected Judgment

- Call your debtor……………………
    - Still in business
    - He/she might actually pay it

STEP TWO: Come to Believe that the Legal Process can Get this judgment Paid
You will need to do your homework.

Come to Believe that the Legal Process Can Get this Judgment Paid

- **Need To Do Your Basic Legal Protection Homework**

    - Do a UCC-1 to determine security interests or banks

    - Make sure your judgment is correctly docketed/recorded

    - Make sure that all steps have been taken to finalize judgment

STEP FIVE: Armed with information, do your Bank, Wage, Merchant or other 3rd party garnishment

Armed With Your Information, Do Your Bank, Wage, Merchant or Other 3rd Party Garnishment

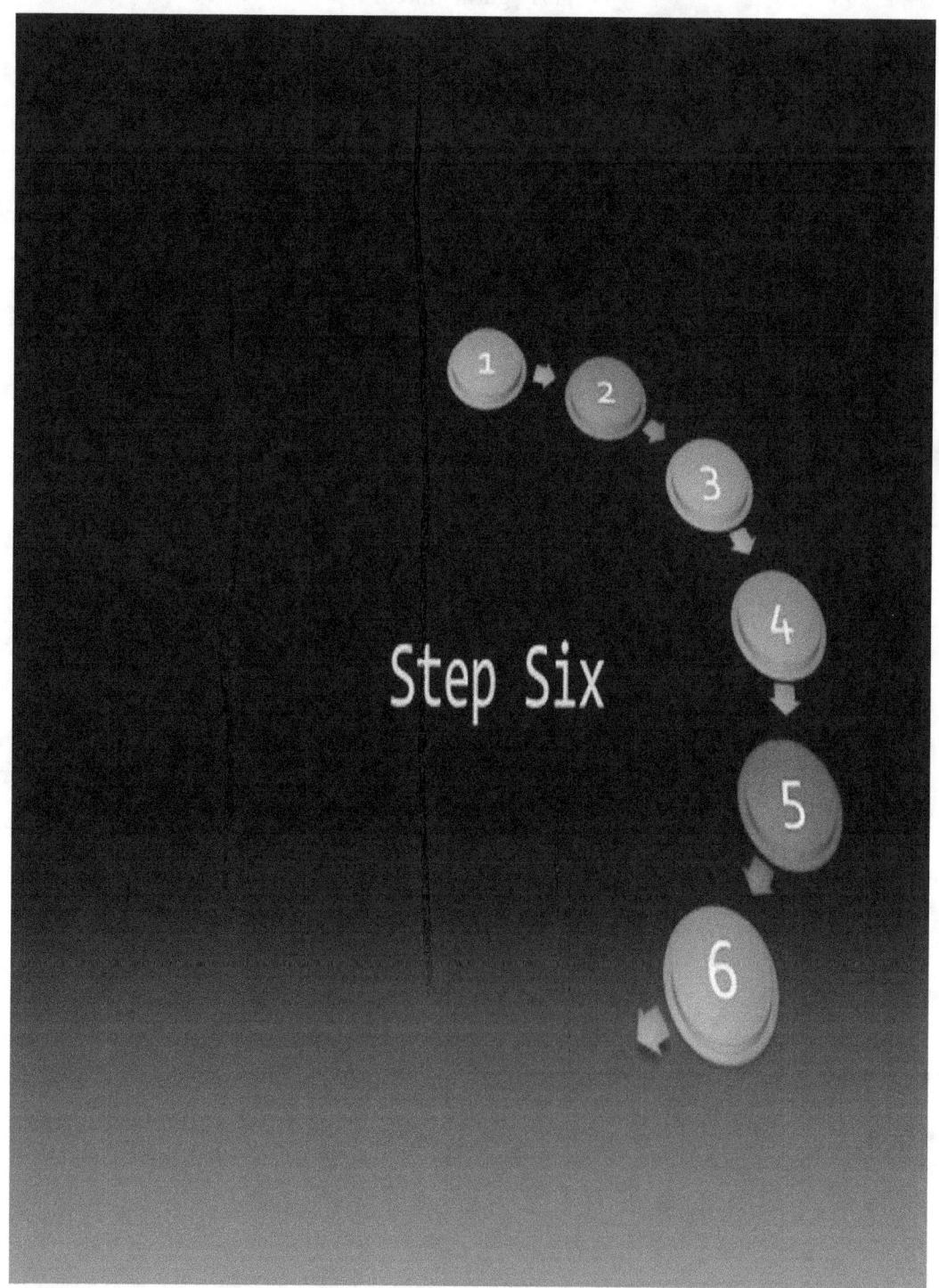

STEP SIX: Submit to your local sheriff

Submit to Your Local Sheriff

- Order execution—Cash Register Levy
- Attach Personal Property
- Pull a Car
- Levy on Real Property
- Make a simple demand for cash

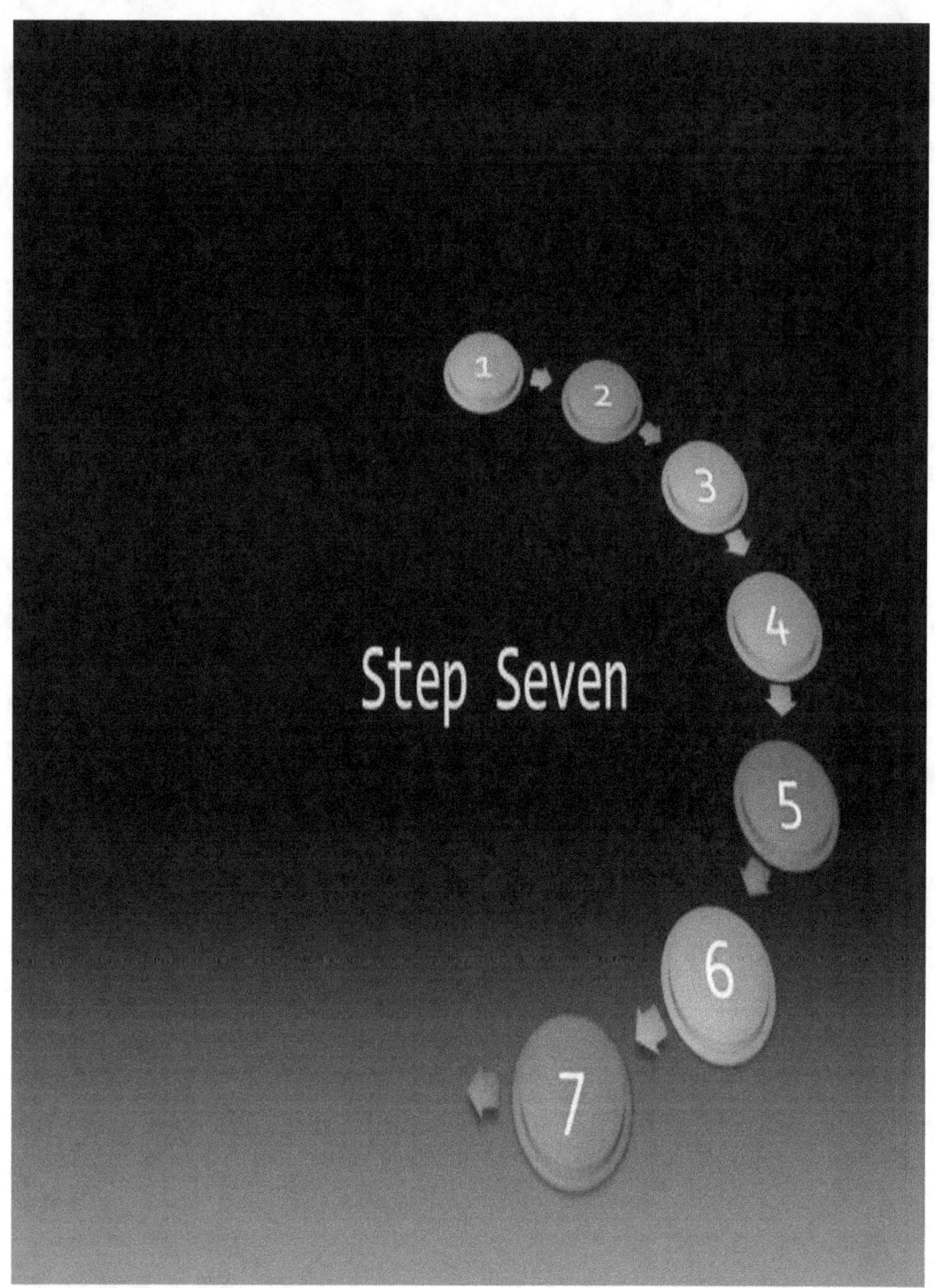

STEP SEVEN: Make a list of Persons/Entities Related to Judgment Debtor and Seek Information

Make a List of Persons/Entities Related to Judgment Debtor and Seek Information

- Banks
- Landlords
- Customers
- Vendors
- Auto Finance Companies
- Mortgage Companies
- Secured Creditors

STEP EIGHT: Make Direct Amends by Using this information to satisfy your judgment

Make Direct Amends by Using This Information to Satisfy Your Judgment

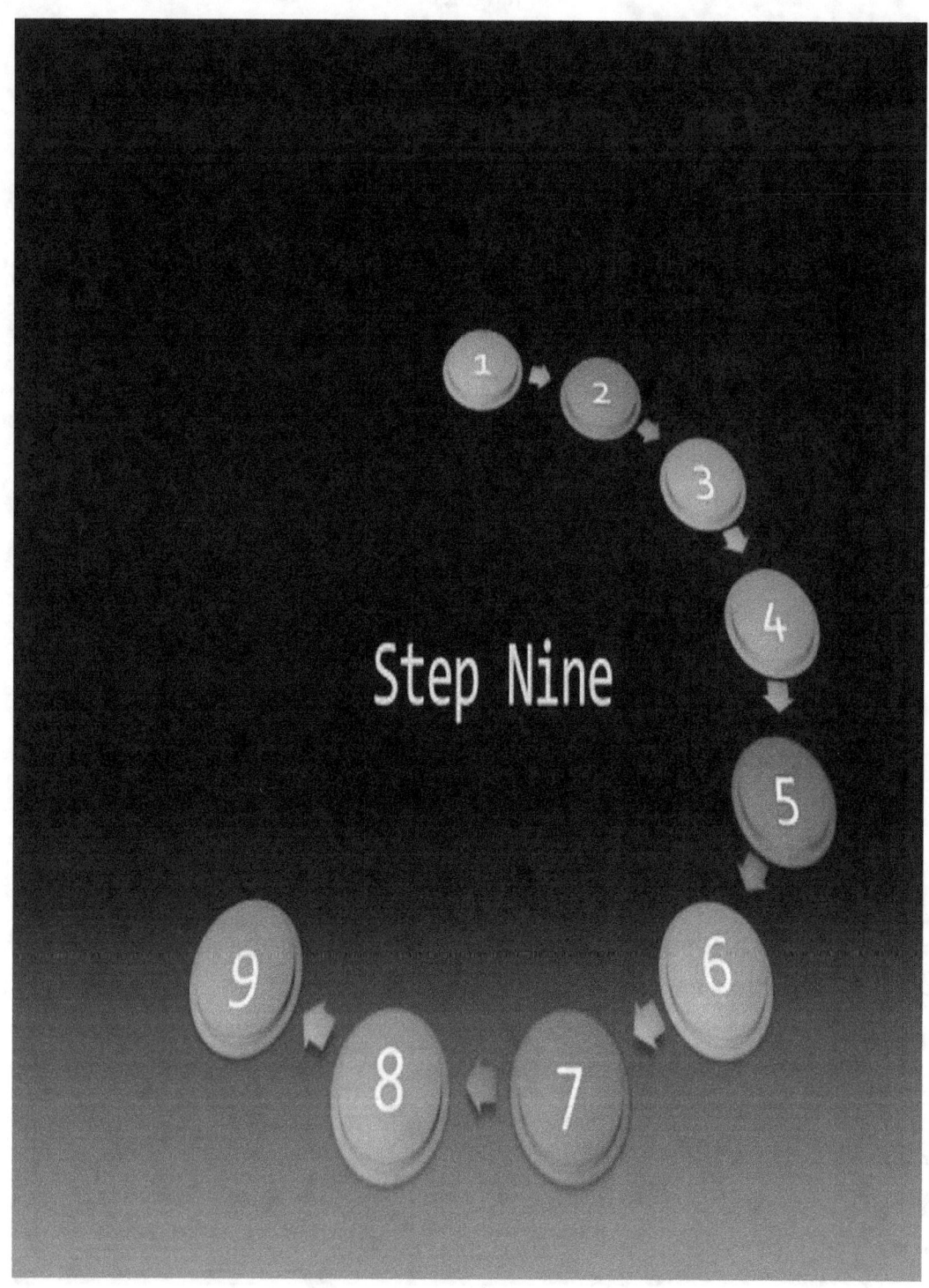

STEP NINE: Humbly Ask the Debtor for Asset Information

Humbly Ask The Debtor For Asset Information

- Schedule a deposition in aid of execution or post judgment discovery

    You are doing this not really for the information you are getting but rather to get a discussion going to get the judgment paid

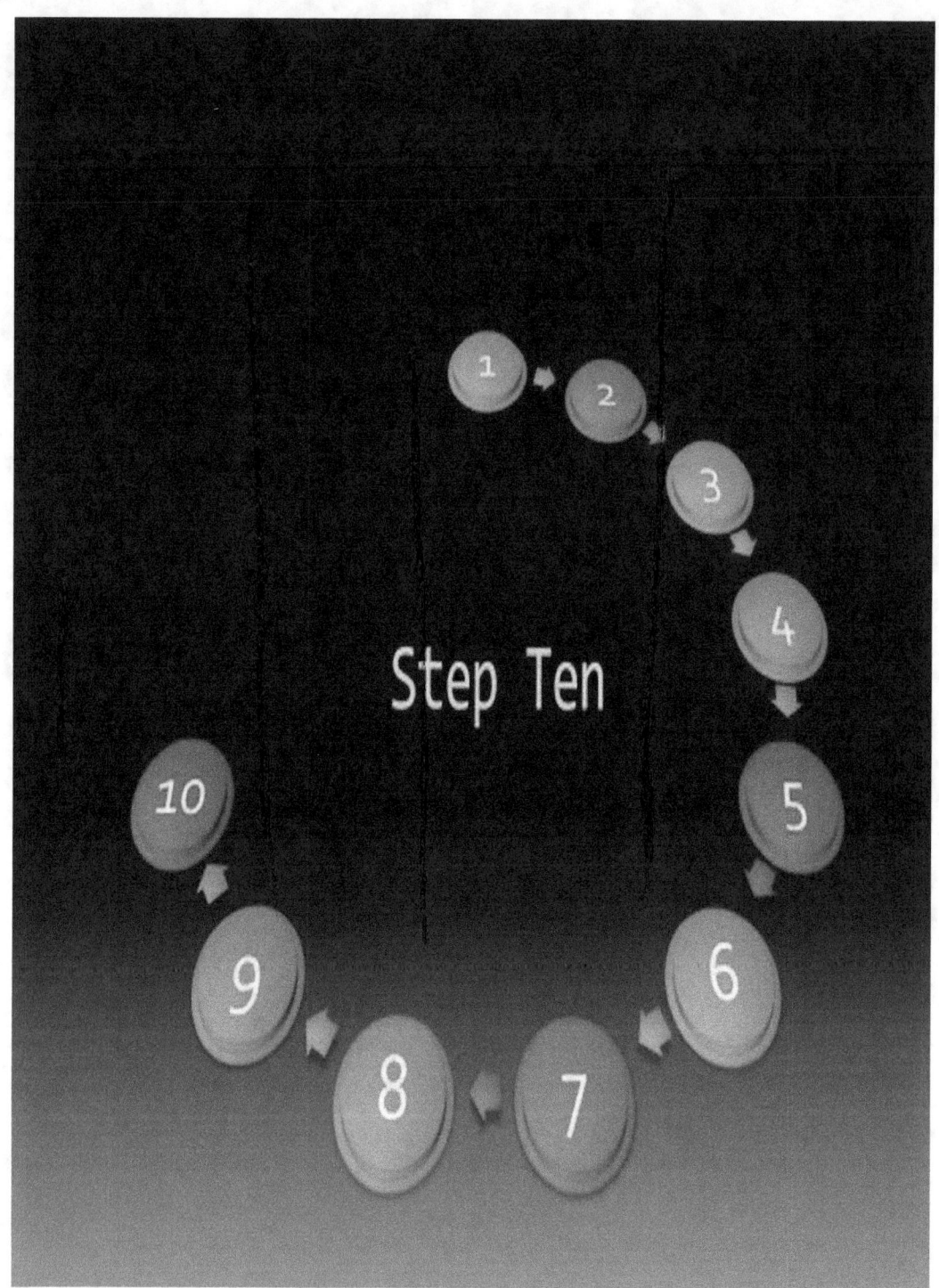

STEP TEN: Continue to Take personal Inventory and consider Extraordinary Methods of Collection

Continue to Take Personal Inventory and Consider Extraordinary Methods of Collection

- Contempt action against the debtor
- Receivership Action
- Involuntary Bankruptcy

STEP ELEVEN : Pray for a Resolution

Pray For A Resolution

- If that does not work..............

    Come back in six months to a year and start the process over again

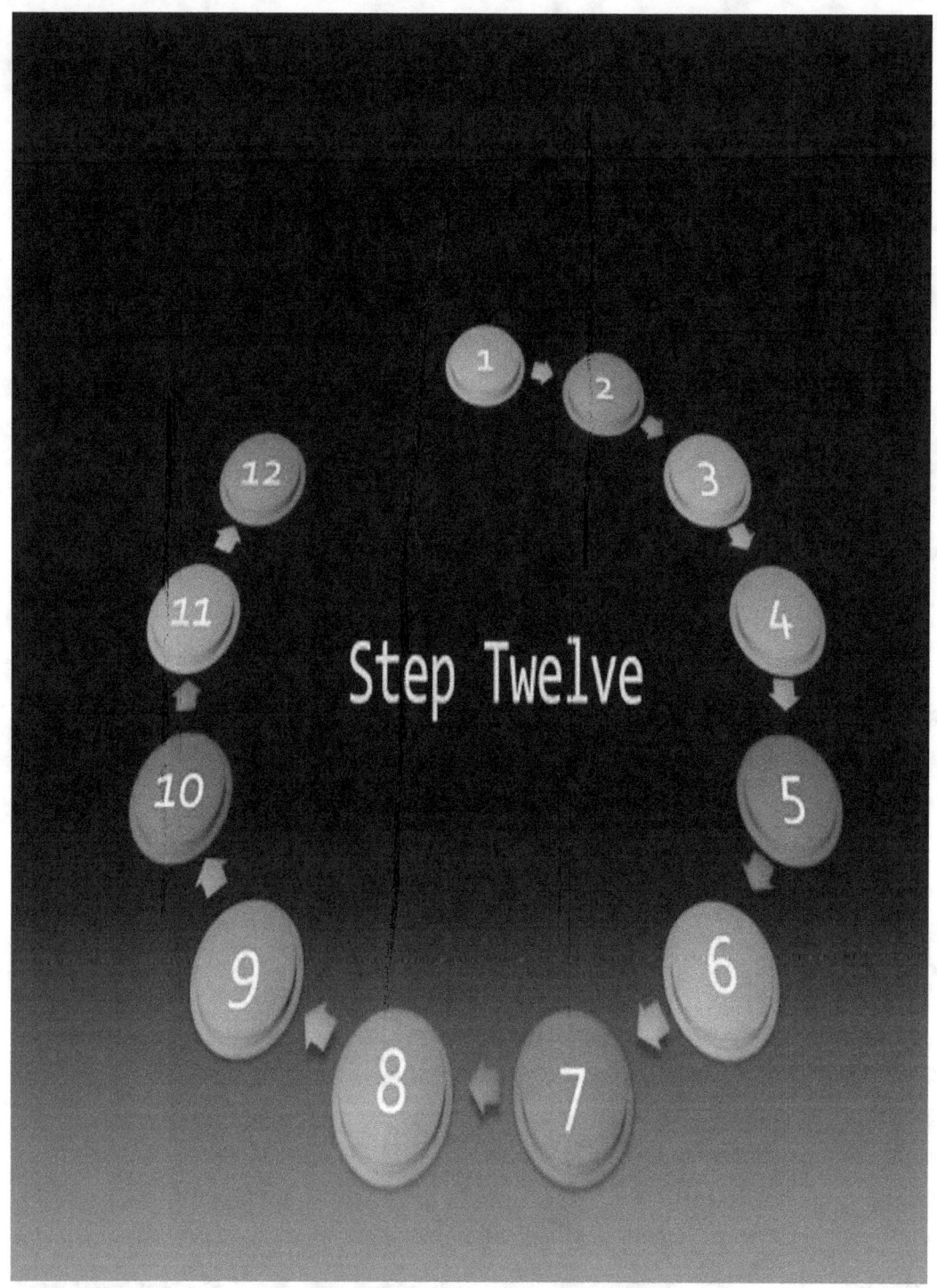

STEP TWELVE: Celebrate in your Collection of the Judgment or Close the file.

Having Had a Spiritual Awaking As a Result of These Steps, Celebrate In Your Collection of The Judgment or Admit Failure and CLOSE THE FILE

www.ingramcontent.com/pod-product-compliance
Lightning Source LLC
Chambersburg PA
CBHW081255180526
45170CB00007B/2428